FANTASTIC

Wreaths

with DALE ROHMAN

NORTH LIGHT BOOKS
AJAX

DEDICATION

I dedicate this book to children everywhere who pick bouquets of dandelions …

To those people who want to add beauty to their lives …

And to my seven grandchildren, Jessica, Ashley and Shaun, Lakin and Rayne, Anna and Emma, who bring beauty into my life every day.

ACKNOWLEDGMENTS

I thank people everywhere who embrace the joy of flowers and allow them to be a part of their everyday lives.

My thanks also to F&W Publications, especially Tricia Waddell, Karen Roberts and Tim Grondin. They are masters in their crafts and were able to transfer my art from the fragility of the real world onto the permanence of the printed page.

From the very depths of my heart I thank Maxine Goldstein, Helen Brandenburg-Barks and Dr. Ronald J. Scott. Each entered my life and changed me for the better. Their acts of kindness, forgiveness and love inspired me not only to grow, but to bloom to my fullest.

A bouquet of thanks to my children, Christian, Martha and Sarah, who are the true flowers of my life. And, above all, my endless thanks to Joan, my bride of thirty-eight years who has always recognized my passion as a gift and encouraged me to share it with others.

07 06 05 04 03   5 4 3 2 1

Library of Congress Cataloging-in-Publication Division

Rohman, Dale L., 1938-
  Fantastic wreaths with Dale Rohman / by Dale Rohman
     p. cm.
  Includes Index
  ISBN 1-58180-289-7 (pbk. : alk. paper)
    1. Wreaths. I. Title.

  TT899.75. R65 2003
  745.92'6–dc21
2002034343

Editor: David Oeters
Designer: Lisa Buchanan
Layout Artist: Kathy Gardner
Production Coordinator: Michelle Ruberg
Photographers: Christine Polomsky and Tim Grondin

ABOUT THE AUTHOR

Known nationally as America's Flower Man, Dale Rohman has created a name for himself over a span of forty successful years in the flower world. Believing that anyone can transform the ordinary into the extraordinary, Dale is an author, speaker and instructor dedicated to sharing his passion for flowers with others.

Appearing in almost every major city in the United States and Canada, Dale is a popular speaker on the Home & Garden, Women's and Flower Show circuits. Dale weaves history, tips, traditions and fascinating folklore as he teaches standing-room-only audiences to create stunning centerpieces using the recycled contents of a junk drawer and incorporating fruits and vegetables into arrangements for distinct designs. Dale's charismatic personality lights up his presentations, and his creations are as unique as the blooms themselves.

Dale has appeared on countless television and radio programs. He regularly shares his floral magic on Home & Garden Television (HGTV) and the Discovery Channel, and has appeared on CNN and NBC's Today show. He has also been featured in magazines and newspapers nationwide.

Believing that flowers can transform lives, Dale developed a hands-on flower-arranging class and luncheon to support the ALS (Lou Gehrig's disease) Association. Taking the event to cities across the country, Dale has raised over one million dollars toward the prevention and cure of the devastating disease.

Dale continues to design through his business, Dale Rohman Enterprises. A specialist in event planning, wedding coordinating, theme parties and the art of entertaining, he has made more than twenty-thousand events come alive with flowers. Dale's unique and innovative designs highlight the individual character of each event. His client list includes some of America's most important corporations and organizations.

Dale lives in St. Louis with his wife, Joan. They have three children and seven grandchildren.

TABLE OF CONTENTS

GIFTS FROM *Nature*

ROMANCE *in Bloom*

CELEBRATE THE *Seasons*

INTRODUCTION

When I was a child, I had an oversized passion, not for baseball or football like the other boys on my block, but for flowers.

My father gave me a small patch of ground behind the garage and said I could plant anything I wanted. He was never disappointed when it didn't turn out to be tomatoes. Zinnias and marigolds flourished for me, and my mother received my bouquets as if they were the most precious flowers on earth. Her tender hugs and kisses of thanks were always followed by her words, "Flowers add beauty to our lives." And so my quest began.

I rooted myself in the floral business because that is what I enjoy doing more than anything in the world. I could not have succeeded in doing anything else. Today, as a professional floral artist, I never allow myself to forget that my art form is more than a livelihood, more than a privilege. It is an awesome gift for which I shall never cease being grateful. And gifts, I believe, are given so that they may be shared.

Throughout my career, friends and clients alike have marveled in amazement at my craft, uttering in the most distressing tone, "I wish I could do that." My immediate response has always been, and continues to be, "You can, and I will show you how."

This book is designed to encourage you. First and foremost, you need to throw out the window any nagging intimidations, and be prepared to stretch your imagination. Dare to be different, and let your creative juices run wild.

Even though there are no set rules to our art, no actual right or wrong design, it is important to adhere firmly to basic arranging techniques. How to properly wire and tape a flower stem, secure a wire pick, make a bow, etc., are all tricks of the trade woven throughout the book, and you will find them extremely easy to learn. These lessons will stay with you forever, and with this know-how you can duplicate what you see on these pages, or per-haps be inspired to take a different creative journey.

Your love for flowers and beauty is obviously as oversized as mine, or you would not have this book in your hand. That makes me happy. You and I are soul mates. Whether you want to hang a wreath on your door to say "Welcome," or hang a silver ellipse on your wall to celebrate a special occa-sion, you can do it! Whether you want to say "Be my Valentine," or surprise a bride-to-be, you can do it! Whether you want to honor the changing sea-sons or dress up your dining room table, you can do it! Go ahead, give it a fling!

Keep in mind: The beauty you bring into your life will certainly rub off on those who surround you. The experience is awesome. I guarantee you will want to repeat the experience again and again.

Laugh at your mistakes and rejoice in your success. Have fun!

ENJOY IN JOY!

Dale

ABOUT WREATHS

Oftentimes, as I take my morning walk, a wreath hanging on someone's front door catches my eye. "Welcome," it says to me. Friendly people surely live there, I fancy.

More and more these days, festive decorations adorn the doors of homes in communities everywhere. Perhaps they are intended to celebrate a special occasion. I like to think they are meant to simply celebrate the day!

I, for one, love to change my door wreath with the changing of the seasons. I feel it's a way of honoring Mother Nature for her awesome sense of mystery and wonder, radiance and magic.

Throughout my professional career, wreaths have remained my favorite expression for my art. One wreath I designed with flowers from the first garden my wife and I shared. It hangs today framed in glass and carries with it fond memories of our youth together.

Wreaths can express patriotism and our love for the world. A recent creation of mine took shape with stalks of natural wheat flaring out four feet in diameter. An entire wreath of mood-moss presented the illusion of rooting the wheat in place, while Old Glory gracefully flowed between the two. Its title: "Amber Waves of Grain."

Wreaths are a visual indication of celebration, expressing and releasing emotions. They were never intended to hang on doors. The ancient Greeks wore them as crowns and chaplets as visual indications of celebration. They were symbols of allegiance, dedication, victory and glory. Winners of all competitions (sport, art, music, poetry) were rewarded with wreaths fashioned from laurel, ivy or pine. The young boys of Greece mocked their heroes, playing with chaplets of roses atop their small heads.

The Romans thought the Greeks effeminate. But it was not long before they adopted the ceremony of placing laurel wreaths on the heads of victorious military warriors. Even chaplets of roses became vogue and were worn by young male Romans when attending councils of the elders before going into battle with the enemy.

Over time, the Romans became obsessed with roses. Lavish crowns were worn by the host and guests alike at the grand banquets and dances of the day. Even the musicians, flute players, dancing girls—the entertainment, along with the working slaves—were elevated in their position with rose crowns of their own.

Greek and Roman lovers practiced the ritual of exchanging crowns when expressing their eternal vows of love and devotion. It soon became a statement of fashion for brides throughout the world to wear wedding wreaths symbolizing their innocence. Crowns of red roses (signifying love and desire) combined with white roses (signifying purity) were a favorite of brides; however, pink roses (beauty and grace) were often mixed with coral roses (meaning, "you are desirable"). The groom encircled his brow as well. Some chose ringlets of grain (fertility) while others wore leaves from the lemon tree (fidelity).

The bridal wreath tradition lingered, and in the nineteenth century, Queen Victoria dared to nestle diamonds in her fragrant crown of orange blossoms. I have long and foolishly dreamed some day to duplicate the Queen's crown for a blushing bride.

The common denominator of all wreaths is that they are handmade. With every wreath, love is the thread that binds it and allows it to last forever, if only in memory. Life gives us plenty of opportunities to hang wreaths on our doors, but perhaps you will agree with me that the best wreath simply celebrates the day.

WREATH FRAMES

Wreath frames are available in many shapes and materials, Styrofoam being the most popular. The designs on the following pages will introduce you to new and different frames and give you an opportunity to construct your very own.

Natural

Natural wreath frames are fashioned from grape and honeysuckle vines, curly-willow branches (sometimes referred to as corkscrew willow), lichen-covered branches and birch tree twigs. Some frames are woven loose and airy, while others are bound tightly to produce a slim appearance. Most styles are available in a variety of sizes.

Styrofoam-Reinforced

Often referred to as a Neilsen frame, these are designed to carry extra weight. Constructed from compressed Styrofoam and reinforced with wire, they ensure maximum support. Sizes range from 10" (25cm) diameter to as large as 48" (122cm) in diameter.

Styrofoam

Soft, light in weight and usually with a beveled edge, Styrofoam is extremely easy to work with. It can be spray painted and is available in sizes that meet most needs.

Floral Foam

Designed to absorb water and retain moisture, floral foam is ideal for fresh cut flowers and foliage. When dry, it works well for lightweight dried and silk flowers. Bands of plastic and a complete backing of plastic ensure support for the foam. Limited sizes are available.

Heart Shapes

Heart shapes come in lightweight and reinforced Styrofoam. They are, however, limited in size and only a few are available with sprayed-on mossy texture.

BASIC TOOLS AND SUPPLIES

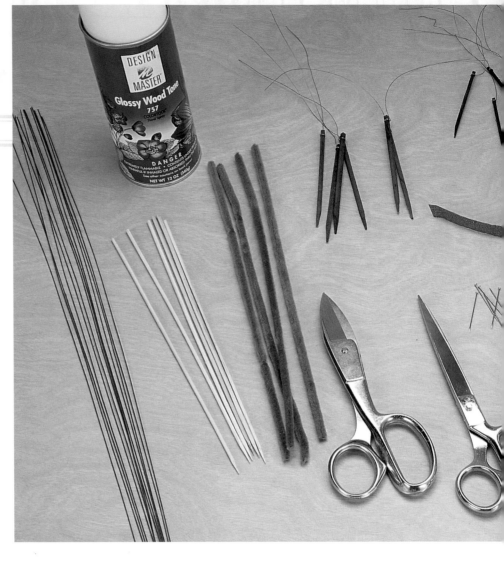

My father used to say, "A man's work is only as good as his tools." Top-of-the-line tools will never desert you; they'll be yours for a lifetime.

Of supplies, my father said, "It's the foundation that makes the house stand!" It's true. Knowing, understanding and using the correct supplies is the foundation for each project in this book.

Wire Cutters

I suggest two wire cutters—one strong pair for cutting floral and chicken wire, and a small lightweight pair for nipping dried and silk flower stems.

Ribbon Shear

Good sharp scissors are necessary for properly cutting ribbon and fabric, and should be used exclusively for that purpose. Cutting paper, cardboard or wire will dull and destroy the blades.

Knife

A good Swiss army knife is a must; it rarely needs sharpening. Use the knife for cutting fresh flowers and foliage only. Cut their stems at a 45° angle, providing a wider space for the stem to draw water. Remember, always cut away from yourself.

Pruning Shears

This is the perfect tool for cutting twigs and natural branches. Get a quality pair at your local hardware store.

Glue Gun

A glue gun is an artisan's best friend! Use it to easily apply fresh, dried and silk flowers, as well as any novelty items. I suggest keeping a bowl of cool water close at hand while using your glue gun. Should the hot glue get on your finger, quickly dip it into the water to prevent a burn.

Floral Wire

The weight of all floral wire is indicated by a gauge number. The smaller the number is, the heavier the weight of the wire; the larger the number is, the lighter the weight of the wire. For the projects in this book, I recommend 22-gauge wire (medium weight).

Floral Paint

Design Master is my paint of choice for all floral needs. Not only are many colors available, but the sprays enhance existing color, dry quickly and do not melt or deform Styrofoam.

Wooden Skewers

These are the perfect extension for securing fruit or vegetables to either Styrofoam or floral foam. It's important to use only natural wood skewers—fruit and vegetables will remain undamaged and can be

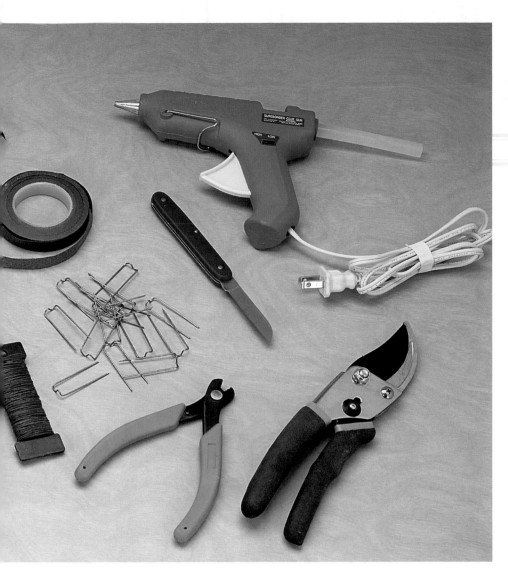

eaten later if so desired. Skewers can be found at your local grocery store.

Chenille Stems

Chenille stems, also known as pipe cleaners, are used in this book as wall hangers. The soft-texture coating around the wire prevents wall scratches. Chenille stems can also substitute for 22-gauge floral wire.

Floral Picks

Wooden floral picks are available in several sizes. Projects require either 3" or 4" (8cm or 10cm) picks. The stick's sharp point gives a tight, permanent hold. When used in wet floral foam, the wood will swell from the moisture, which also increases the holding power. The picks are perfect for extending stem lengths and securing individual items into clusters.

Floral Tape

Although floral tape is available in a variety of colors, dark green and brown will serve our purposes. When wrapped around floral wire, the tape acts as a camouflage, and the somewhat sticky texture of the tape increases the wire's holding power. When using the wooden floral pick, I recommend applying floral tape to ensure additional firmness.

Floral Pins

Sometimes referred to as "greening pins" or "philly pins," floral pins secure stems, artificial garlands, twigs, etc., to Styrofoam and floral foam bases. Insert two pins per stem from opposite directions at a 45° angle for the strongest holding power.

Paddle Wire

Known also as spool wire, paddle wire allows for continuous wiring and is perfect for garland making and adhering foliage, flowers, etc., to a preexisting wire frame.

BASIC TECHNIQUES

Adding a Wired Floral Pick to a Stem
The most important purpose for this technique is to provide a sharp point to any blunt-end stems (artificial or natural) and clusters of berries, candies, etc. It is the sharp point that will hold the stem or cluster firmly into foam (in the wet foam, the wooden pick will swell and expand from the moisture, which is an added means of security). Because the wire picks are available in several lengths, additional length can be added to any stem that may have been mistakenly cut too short. Once the pick is wired into place, cover the wired area with floral tape.

Creating a Chenille Hanger
The chenille (pipe cleaner) hanger is ideal for wreaths and swags made on a foam base. Once the wire pick is added, cover the wired area with floral tape for additional security. Before you place the hanger on the back side of the foam, dot the point of the wooden pick with hot glue, then insert the pick at a 45° angle. Allow the glue to dry to be sure the pick is firm, then gently twist the chenille loop upright for proper hanging.

one

two

1 Hold the wired pick parallel to the flower stem.

2 Make the first twist of the wire above the wood pick and onto the flower stem only. Continue twisting down the stem and the pick, securing the two together. Make the last twist below the stem and only onto the wooden pick.

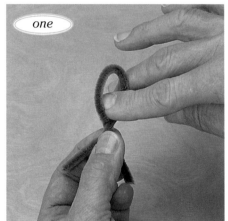

one

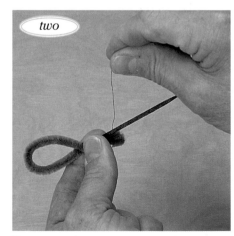

two

1 Cut a chenille stem (pipe cleaner) in half and twist into a loop. Cut off the excess stem.

2 Take a 3" or 4" (8cm or 10cm) wired floral pick and twist it around the twisted end of the chenille loop. Add a wire pick to secure the hanger to the wreath.

TIPS AND TRICKS FOR CARING FOR YOUR WREATH

Most likely you will choose a location for your wreath long before you begin to make it. My tip is to be sure to select materials that will be best suited for that area. For example, outdoor wreaths are better made from the weather experienced treasures of mother nature: twigs and branches, cones and berries. Certainly silk and artificial flowers and foliage can be added, provided there is some overhead protection to ward off intense rain and extensive bright light, both of which can prove very damaging.

With indoor wreaths, however, you need not be so apprehensive. Feel comfortable working with any fragile and delicate dried and/or silk flowers. I do recommend, however, that you do not hang your wreath on doors that are in constant use. Slamming doors prove very abusive unless you secure your wreath firmly, not only at the top, but at the bottom as well. It's best also to keep the wreath away from areas of excessive moisture, humidity and direct sunlight, and out of reach of investigating pets. After time, particles of dust can be removed with gentle strokes of a small artist brush.

To store your wreath, place it in an oversized dark plastic trash bag and keep it in a hanging position. I also suggest that, before you bag your wreath, you tuck small wads of tissue into the loops of ribbons and bows to help retain their shape.

Fresh flower wreaths, of course, are best made just before the celebration for which they are intended. The morning of the occasion is my suggestion; however, if you are using a wet-foam frame and have a means of storing it in a cool area (42°F {6°C}), the day before is perfect. In either case, it is necessary to let the wreath hang for at least twenty minutes in the work area to allow the excess water to drip from the foam. Once hung in its designated location, periodic misting is helpful.

My prize tip, my supreme trick, is simply to treat your wreath with the same love and respect you show all your other special treasures and it can last a lifetime.

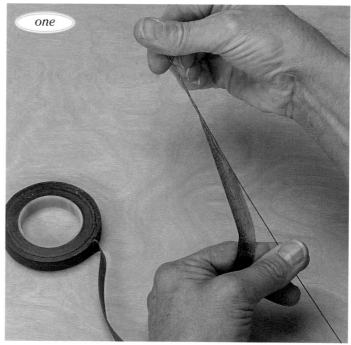

one

1 Twist the floral tape firmly at one end of the wire. Twist the tape around and down the wire at a 45° angle. Stretch the tape as you pull and twist.

Taping Florist Wire

Florist wire is slick and therefore sometimes difficult to twist firmly. Covering the wire with floral tape provides a tacky texture that creates a stronger, tighter hold. Because florist wire is always green and floral tape is available in a variety of colors (two shades of green, brown, twig and numerous pastels) you have the advantage of choosing the tape color that will allow you to conceal or camouflage the area you are wiring.

"Nature is man's teacher. She unfolds her treasures to his search, unseals his eyes, illumes his mind, and purifies his heart; an influence breathes from all the sights and sounds of her existence."

GIFTS FROM *Nature*

These words were penned by the American author Alfred Billings Street (1811-1881). Selfishly, I like to feel Mr. Street wrote them strictly with me in mind. How often I have stepped from my stoop into a world of unbelievable treasures; how often my mind has been set wheeling into creativity from what my eyes were unsealed to see; how often that creativity has been influenced by the sights and sounds that exist in the gifts of nature. Every morsel, every fragment and snippet of nature's vast collection of wonder is a delicacy to savor. And to those of us who so love our craft, nature is calling "come help yourself, use my beauty to enrich your own." The designs on the upcoming pages are the magical results of my personal response to the call of the natural world. Hopefully they will encourage you to search, listen, see and be influenced by all that is available as a gift from nature.

SWEET AND SOUR

Lemons aren't just for lemonade anymore! Greet your summertime guests with good-taste decorating. A pinch of sweet and a dash of sour can stir up the perfect party mood for any lazy, hazy day of summer. If perishable materials are not your first choice, this project can be duplicated with artificial foliages and lemons.

MATERIALS LIST

· 10 lemons · butterscotch candy · 1 stem of silk white hydrangea blossoms · ½ bunch of fresh lemon leaves · ½ bunch of fresh seeded eucalyptus · 15" (38cm) floral foam wreath base · · floral wire (optional) · floral tape · ten 3" (8cm) wire picks · · glue gun · 20 wooden skewers · chenille stems ·

TURN FRESH LEMONS INTO LEMON PIE

Give the lemons in your wreath a second life by turning them into this delicious summertime dessert.

Lemon Angel Pie

Meringue shell:
3 egg whites
½ tsp. cream of tartar
I cup sugar

Beat egg whites with cream of tartar in a medium-sized bowl until foamy. Beat in the sugar, a tablespoon at a time, until the meringue forms stiff glossy peaks. Lightly butter a 9-inch pie plate. Spoon the meringue over the bottom and high up the sides to form a shell. Bake in an oven at 275°F (135°C) for I hour. Turn off the oven; leave meringue in oven until cool.

Lemon filling:

5 egg yolks
⅔ cup sugar
I tbsp. grated lemon rind
⅓ cup lemon juice, freshly squeezed
I cup heavy cream, whipped
Lemon slices and mint leaves, optional

Beat egg yolks in top of a double boiler until frothy. Beat in the sugar slowly until mixture is thick and light. Stir in lemon rind and lemon juice. Cook, stirring constantly, over hot, not boiling water until filling is thick, about I2 to I4 minutes; cool thoroughly. Spoon cooled filling into meringue shell; cover loosely. Refrigerate at least I2 hours. Top with whipped cream; decorate with lemon slices and mint, if desired.

1 Cut at an angle 2" and 4" (5cm and 10cm) sprigs of lemon leaves. Insert them in the foam wreath until you achieve full coverage.

2 Cut 4" and 6" (10cm and 15cm) sprigs of seeded eucalyptus. Insert them throughout the foam wreath.

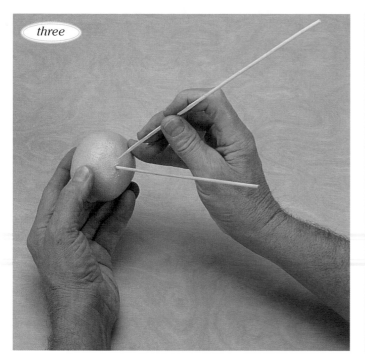

three

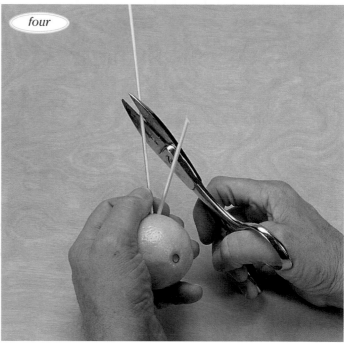

four

five

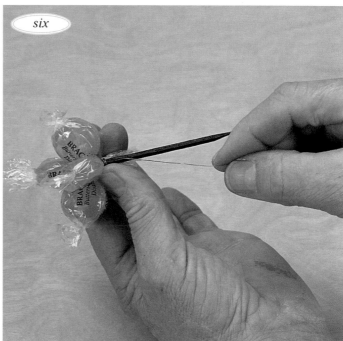

six

3 Insert two wooden skewers into a lemon in a Y-shape.

4 Cut the wooden skewers into 3" (8cm) lengths.

5 Repeat steps three and four for all lemons. Insert five clusters of two lemons into the wreath.

6 Select four butterscotch candies and twist a 3" (8cm) wire pick around the ends of the wrapped candy.

[21]

seven

eight

nine

7 Wrap floral tape around the pick.

8 Repeat steps six and seven to make ten butterscotch clusters, and insert two butterscotch clusters at each lemon cluster.

9 Cut individual white flowers from the hydrangea stem. Glue them randomly throughout the wreath. Create a hanger with a chenille stem (see Basic Techniques, page 14).

TIPS FOR KEEPING
A BEAUTIFUL WREATH

The question I am most asked regarding wreath care is, "How do I keep my dried flowers and materials from shedding?" My one-word reply is always "hairspray"! Even with a wreath such as this, a generous application of hairspray will act as a glue of sorts and keep even the tiniest blossoms secure to their stems. I recommend you only spray once the wreath is completed, and never spray a wreath whose fruits you might eat. Remember, don't be stingy with the spray. Coat both the front and the back of the wreath.

DESIGNER'S TIP

If you use artificial materials, be sure to select two varieties of foliage for texture and color, and lemons that are about the same size as the fresh. Begin with a green spray-painted Styrofoam wreath frame and then follow the usual instructions. In place of skewers, however, you will need 19-gauge floral wire and an ice pick. Carefully poke a hole in each side of the plastic lemon with the ice pick, thread the 19-gauge floral wire through, and twist the ends together. Add a 3" (8cm) floral pick to the wire end, and wrap with floral tape. The advantage of your nonperishable wreath? The "sweet" is still sweet and the "sour" has no juice!

FRESH TO EVERLASTING

A wreath of roses symbolizes love, joy and remembrance. When you use fresh roses, the delicate fragrance of this wreath is sure to linger, adding even more magic to a romantic celebration. Arranged fresh and in full bloom, the queen of flowers will dry, and the memories of romantic celebrations will live forever.

MATERIALS LIST

· 30 fresh white "message" roses · 1 stem fresh limonium
("sunglow blue") · ½ bunch lemon leaves (salal) ·
· 15" (38cm) floral foam wreath base · knife ·
· 22-gauge floral wire ·

① Cut 2" to 4" (5cm to 10cm) sprigs, at an angle, from a half bunch of lemon leaves.

② The floral foam wreath base should be submerged under water until the tiny "bubbles" disappear, ensuring complete saturation. (This allows the short stems of the roses and lemon leaves to rapidly absorb the water, making them last longer.) Insert the lemon leaf sprigs into the presoaked floral foam wreath. Cover the entire wreath.

③ Cut about thirty white roses with 1½" (4cm) stems. Be sure to cut them at an angle. The roses should be at various stages of development. Insert the roses throughout the wreath at different angles. You do not want a smooth appearance.

④ Cut the rose foliage, and insert it throughout the wreath.

five

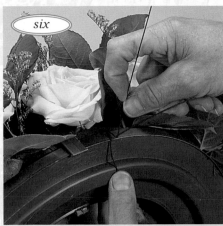

six

5. Cut one stem of limonium into many sprigs with 2" (5cm) stems. Insert them randomly throughout the wreath.

6. Insert the floral wire into the plastic base of the wreath, twist the ends together then twist onto the edge of the plastic.

7. Twist the ends of the floral wire to make a hook. Cut off the excess.

seven

DESIGNER'S TIP

Your wreath's fresh appearance should last two days, then the "everlasting" process will begin. The wreath will slowly dry as the moisture evaporates from the foam. Expect the roses to change color somewhat and the lemon leaves to fade and possibly curl. Once the wreath is brittle to the touch, spray it generously with hairspray for protection. To duplicate the rose wreath with artificial flowers, begin with a Styrofoam wreath frame spray-painted green, and then follow the instructions as listed.

TASTE OF AUTUMN

The hues of harvest are served in abundant portions. Reap those that are most unexpected. Foliage, fruits and vegetables of contrasting colors create a tasty wreath that will not only welcome, but also glorify the season of plenty. Copperbeach is a natural foliage treated with an oil and dye, giving it an endless life span. If its color doesn't suit you, feel free to substitute an artificial fall-flavored foliage.

MATERIALS LIST

· 3 Granny Smith apples · 7 banana peppers · 3 limes ·

· 6 stems of fresh limonium · 1 bunch of fresh copperbeach foliage ·

· 3 yards (2.7m) of 1½"-wide (3.8cm) light green satin double-faced
wire ribbon · 16" (41cm) foam wreath frame · 26 wooden skewers ·

· chenille stems · floral tape (optional) · glue gun ·

· green spray paint · three 4" (10cm) wire picks ·

1 Spray-paint the foam wreath green.

2 Cut the copperbeach into 5" (13cm) sprigs. Insert the sprigs throughout the wreath until it is fully covered.

3 Cut the wooden skewers at an angle into 4" (10cm) pieces. Insert two skewers, in a Y-shape, into a Granny Smith apple. Repeat on two more apples. Make a cluster with two of the apples and insert them into the wreath. Insert the third apple diagonally across from the cluster.

four

five

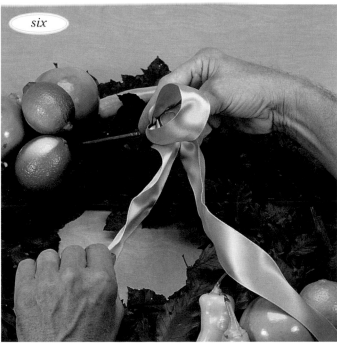

six

4 Insert two 4" (10cm) skewers into a banana pepper. Repeat on six more peppers. Insert five peppers around one apple cluster, and two peppers around the other.

5 Insert two 4" (10cm) skewers into a lime. Repeat for the two others. Insert two limes next to the five-pepper cluster and one lime next to the two-pepper cluster.

6 Cut 1 yard (91cm) of 1½"-wide (4cm) ribbon. Fold the ribbon in two lengthwise and pinch the ribbon to create a loop and two streamers. Make one of the streamers longer than the other. Wrap a 4" (10cm) wire pick around the ribbon loop, and insert it into the larger cluster of fruits and vegetables.

seven

7 Cut another 1-yard (91cm) piece of ribbon, and fold it into four loops (two on each side). Wrap a 4" (10cm) wire pick around the center of the bow.

8 Insert the bow into the wreath, above the larger fruit and vegetable cluster.

eight

THE FIRST GARDEN

I'll never forget the experience of my first garden. As a "rookie-gardener" at age eight, I– like the tender seed sprouts poking through the soil– was green and unsure of the growing process. "Love and water," my father encouraged, would allow the sprouts to shoot upward and explode into magnificent blooms of many colors, sizes and shapes. My flowers were an easy victory. But by the end of that first summer, I realized the many colors, sizes and shapes were fleeting rapidly and disappointment set in. The blooms were not going to last, as I had hoped, forever. "Not to worry," my father continued to advise, "you can dry them and they'll last as long as you want them to." My victory was exonerated.

Drying flowers, though an ancient practice, was an exciting new adventure for me then and still is to this day.

nine

ten

9 Cut more 5" (13cm) sprigs of copper-beach, and insert it to cover the skewers. Cut 1-yard (91cm) of ribbon and make another two-loop bow, using a 4" (10cm) wire pick wrapped around the bow's center. Insert the bow into the wreath above the large fruit and vegetable cluster.

10 Cut sprigs of limonium into 4" and 6" (10cm and 15cm) lengths. Insert the shorter sprigs near the clusters of fruit and vegetables, and the longer throughout. Create a hanger with a chenille stem.

DESIGNER'S TIP

If you'd rather not use fresh produce, artificial works just as well. Instead of using wooden skewers, use 19-gauge floral wire and an ice pick to secure the fruits and vegetables to the Styrofoam wreath frame. Carefully poke a hole into each side of the fruit or vegetable with the ice pick. Thread the 19-gauge wire through and twist the ends together; add a wire floral pick and wrap with floral tape. Follow the usual placement instructions. Your wreath will glorify the season of plenty in good taste to be sure.

MOSTLY MOSS

Gifts from Mother Earth easily add color and warmth to the dreary, bleak and cold days of winter. Lichen, moss, berries and rose hips, fluidly molded into an uninterrupted flow, bring life to a black-and-white winter world. Experiment with different clusters of dried flowers (or even silk), allowing the wreath to change with the seasons—perhaps use sunflowers in summertime, wheat and/or gourds for fall. The choices are endless.

MATERIALS LIST

· sheet moss · mood moss · reindeer moss · lichen ·
· 1 bunch of tallow berries (popcorn berries) ·
· 1 bunch of rose hips · 7 dried Venus flytraps (sarracena) ·
· 18" (46cm) wire reinforced foam wreath ·nineteen 4" (10cm) wire
picks · floral tape · floral pins · chenille stems ·

one

two

1. Dampen the sheet moss, and attach it to the foam wreath with floral pins. Cover the wreath completely. Dampen the mood moss, and insert it in clusters with floral pins throughout the wreath.

2. Dampen the reindeer moss and lichen, and insert them throughout the wreath with floral pins.

three

four

3. Attach a 4" (10cm) wire pick to a small cluster of rose hips. Wrap the pick with floral tape. Make a total of six small clusters. Insert two of the clusters opposite each other at 45° angles (in a Y-shape), forming one larger cluster. Repeat twice, for a total of three large clusters. Place them at the top and bottom of the wreath, and on one side. Leave one corner open for the flytraps.

4. Attach four small clusters of tallow berries to 4" (10cm) wire picks, and insert them between the rose hip clusters.

five

six

5 Wrap seven Venus flytraps with a 4"
   (10cm) wire pick.

6 Insert the flytraps into the wreath at a 45°
   angle.

7 Attach 4" (10cm) wire picks to two more
   rose hip clusters, and insert them on
   either side of the Venus flytrap bunch at
   45° angles. Create a hanger with a chenille stem.

seven

DESIGNER'S TIP

_Mother Earth is a natural trendsetter, and
moss never goes out of style. Therefore,
treat your moss wreath as you would a
basic black dress. In the simplicity of its
natural state, it is elegant. Yet with the
right accessories, it can be elevated to a
more sophisticated level. Tuck in sprigs of
fresh holly for the Christmas season, and
to really dress it up, touch it off with a few
small but sparkling bangles and beads._

ECHOES OF GARDEN PAST

Christian Nestell Bovee said, "To cultivate a garden is to walk with God." Gardening is a labor of love and every beautiful bloom becomes a triumph, a precious prize, a statement of victory. Displaying these gifts of beauty for all to see is of the essence. What better way can the love and passion of a gardener be shared?

MATERIALS LIST

· 1 bunch of dried roses · 1 bunch of dried spray roses ·
· 1 bunch of dried bittersweet · 1 bunch of dried hydrangea ·
· 1 bunch of dried sea foam statice · 1 bunch of dried cockscomb
(celosia) · 1 bunch of dried global anthus · 12 bamboo sticks,
each 21" (53cm) long · floral tape · 22-gauge wire · raffia · 1½-yards
(1.4m) of 1½"-wide (4cm) pink double-faced satin ribbon · hairspray ·

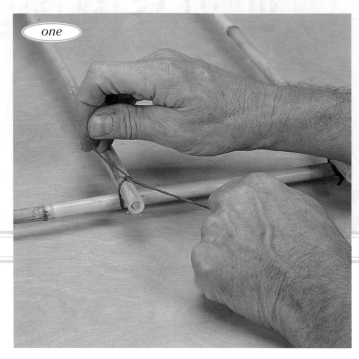

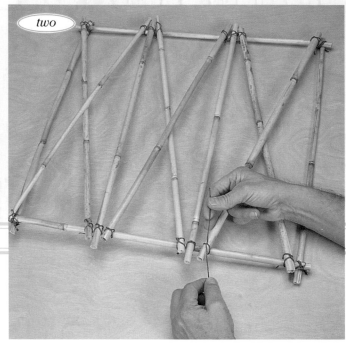

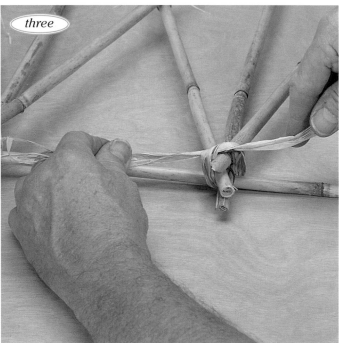

1. Cut twelve bamboo sticks to 21" (53cm) long each. Lay out four in a square, and use 22-gauge wire wrapped in floral tape to secure each corner. Place two pieces of bamboo vertically across the square, dividing it into even thirds. Secure with 22-gauge wire. Crisscross the wire and twist it in the back. Cut off the excess.

2. Take six bamboo sticks and make three Xs in the center of the bamboo stick square. Twist 22-gauge wire wrapped in floral tape to secure each end. Crisscross the wire and twist at the back. Cut off the excess.

3. Cut four strands of 12" to 18" (31cm to 46cm) raffia, and tie it around the intersections of the bamboo sticks. Repeat at each place where wire secures the sticks. Cut off the excess raffia.

4. Tie small bunches of dried roses, dried spray roses, dried bittersweet, dried sea foam statice, dried cockscomb, dried hydrangea and dried anthus with 22-gauge wire wrapped in floral tape. Wrap raffia over the wire, and attach the bunches to the bamboo frame. Tie some of the raffia in knots around the flower bunches, and tie some of the raffia in bows. Apply hairspray to prevent shedding.

five

six

5 Cut 1½ yards (1.4m) of pink satin ribbon. String the ribbon through the bamboo stick perimeter, and tie a shoestring bow. Allow the bow streamers to hang into the bamboo frame.

6 To make a hanger, take a handful of full-length raffia (about two yards or 1.8m) and knot it at each end. Make two knots in the middle. Use 22-gauge wire wrapped in floral tape to attach the raffia to the bamboo frame. Cover the wire with a small piece of raffia.

USING DRIED FLOWERS

Rather than using fresh flowers on the frame, I recommend air-drying them first. Select your flowers and/or grasses preferably on a clear, dry day. Assemble the flowers into small bunches, leaving the stems as long as possible. Tie each bunch tightly with twine. Hang the bunches upside down in a cool, dark, dry area. Drying should take about two weeks. Once done, they're yours forever.

DESIGNER'S TIP

If you are fortunate enough to have an overly abundant crop of dried flowers, you may decide to create a much larger bamboo frame. Or, you may also accommodate your abundance with several smaller frames, and present them as gifts to those who love your garden as much as you do.

MONARCHS IN FLIGHT

Celebrate the summer season by honoring the miracle of the monarchs. As a symbol of new life, spirited and playful butterflies encourage, "Come fly with me. Today is the first day of the rest of your life." This wreath, for me, becomes a symbol of freedom. With a minor change in the flower choice, you can hang this remarkable display year-round as a cheerful memory that when summer returns, so will nature's miracles.

MATERIALS LIST

· 1 large monarch · 12 small monarchs · 3 sprays of golden waffle ·

· 2 sprays of artificial forsythia · 1 bunch of lichen-covered branches ·

· floral tape · 22-gauge wire ·

one

two

three

four

1 Use 22-gauge wire to arrange 18" (46cm) lichen-covered branches into a pentagon-shaped wreath.

2 Repeat the first step. Use floral wire to attach the second pentagon to the original pentagon frame, slightly shifting the corners. Repeat to create the depth and height that you desire.

3 Take the sprays of golden waffle and twist the stems into corkscrews. Secure them to the wreath with a 6" (15cm) piece of 22-gauge wire wrapped in floral tape. Place all three sprays on the left side of the wreath.

4 Insert two sprays of forsythia into the wreath by tucking them into the lichen-covered branches. Cut off the excess stems. Secure the forsythia to the branches with 22-gauge wire wrapped in floral tape. Pull the wire taut then cut the excess.

five

six

5. Glue the large butterfly to the right and bottom of the wreath.

6. Glue twelve small butterflies to the wreath. Place most of them in the lower left section.

DESIGNER'S TIP

Hang your wreath in an area where it will always be in full view, a constant reminder of the freedom we are all so fortunate to embrace. If you like, change the artificial flower sprays with the changing of the seasons—sunflowers in summer, oak leaves or thistles in fall, pine boughs in winter.

"In this commonplace world

everyone is said to be romantic

who either admires a finer thing or does one."

ROMANCE

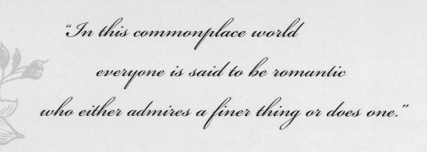

in Bloom

These are the words of English poet Alexander Pope (1688-1744) and they continuously inspire me—and I hope they will inspire you as well, to create with passion and zeal, joy and beauty. I strongly believe romance never goes out of style. And in no way can we have too much of it in our lives. How fortunate are we to be able, through our craft, to bring into bloom the romance that overwhelms us to share freely our feelings and emotions not only with those who surround us in our daily lives, but surely romantics of the future. The designs on the following pages are some expressions of the blooming abundance within me. I freely share them with you. Although they are presented to be duplicated, allow yourself your own freedom. Let your emotions bloom and blossom into a romance that can only be a continuance of the love that is already within you. BLOOM!

RING AROUND THE ROSY

Tagore once said, "Truth smiles when she beholds her own face in a perfect mirror." I say, "Mirror, mirror on the wall, be the fairest of them all. Rings of beauty fashion a frame, around the face of beauty the same." What a delightful and unique gift this charming wreath could be, especially for that very special young lady about to turn sweet sixteen.

MATERIALS LIST

· 1 bunch of prepared eucalyptus · 7 sprays of dried silk rosebuds
(25-30 rosebuds) · 12 clusters of dried pepper berries ·
· 8" (20cm) mirror · 10" (25cm) wreath with a moss coat and
wire-reinforced · wire clothes hanger · floral pins ·
· 24-gauge paddle wire · 22-gauge wire · glue gun ·

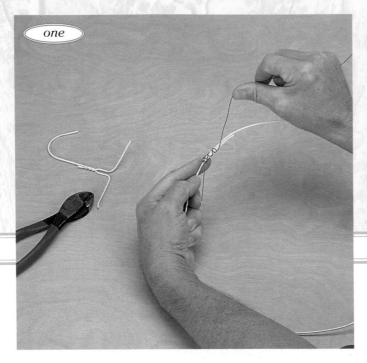

one

two

three

four

1. Cut off the head of the hanger. Form a circle that is a bit bigger than the wreath, overlapping the ends of the hanger. Wrap a 22-gauge floral wire over the overlapped section. At the end of the section, wrap the wire back over it in the opposite direction so it is double wired.

2. Cut 2½" to 3" (6cm to 8cm) sprigs of prepared eucalyptus. Use 24-gauge paddle wire to connect them to the hanger ring. Add two pieces at a time. Don't cut the wire until you get to the end.

3. Place the eucalyptus ring around the moss wreath. Secure with floral pins.

4. Glue the mirror to the back of the moss wreath.

five

six

5. Cut off the stems of the dried silk rosebuds so you have twenty-five to thirty rosebuds, and glue them all the way around the moss wreath's outer edge.

6. Cut six rose leaves, and glue them evenly around the rosebuds.

7. Glue twelve clusters of pepper berries along the inner edge of the moss wreath. Cut off the berry stems if they are too long.

seven

DESIGNER'S TIP

You may wish to alter the colors of this wreath, but I don't suggest changing its size, which is very much a part of its charm. You can add to that charm by daring to be different and hanging it in an unexpected area. It will bring an air of enchantment to the powder room or guest bedroom, or stand out in all its glory when hung as a part of a collection of other mirrors. The hall or stairway will become a much more important part of the house if graced with its presence. Move it around the house until your "rosy" is "cozy"!

SILVER ELEGANCE

Every day should be celebrated as though it were a silver jubilee. The splendor of an illustrious ellipse can serve as a constant reminder of "finding the silver lining," as well as displaying a show of joy. This project uses prepared eucalyptus, which is available in numerous colors. You may want to use a more neutral color so you'll have more options for changing the ellipse with the seasons.

MATERIALS LIST

· ½ bunch of prepared eucalyptus · 1 bunch of tallow berries ·

· ½ bunch of dried silver brunia · 6 dried roses ·

· 1 yard (91cm) of ⅝" (2cm) white grosgrain ribbon ·

· wire clothes hanger · 22-gauge wire ·

· 24-gauge paddle wire · glue gun ·

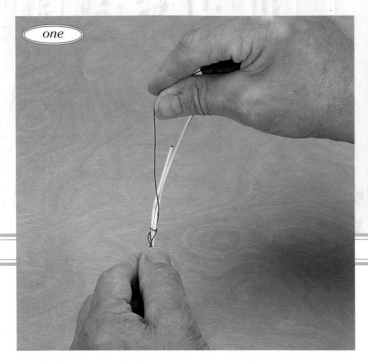

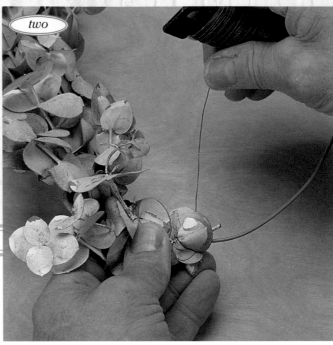

one

two

three

1 Cut the hanger at the head, and wrap it with 22-gauge wire to form a 12" x 7½" (31cm x 19cm) oval.

2 Cut the eucalyptus in 3" to 4" (8cm to 10cm) sprigs, and wrap them two at a time with paddle wire to the hanger.

3 Glue the tallow berries and silver brunia throughout the oval wreath.

four

five

4. Glue dried rose buds in clusters of two throughout the wreath. Glue the rose petals throughout also.

5. To make the hanger, cut 1 yard (91cm) of grosgrain ribbon, and tie a knot on each end. Wrap the ribbon through the top of the wreath and glue to secure.

DESIGNER'S TIP

Planning an elegant sit-down dinner party? Remove your silver ellipse from the wall, and place it in the center of the dining room table. A mirror underneath will add to the elegance. A three-branch silver candelabra or a grouping of crystal candlesticks placed on the mirror will create an instant centerpiece you can be very proud of. Of course, to be effective, your ellipse need not be silver; use any color that best suits your décor.

THREE'S COMPANY

Triple your pleasure, triple your fun, three charming wreaths, cascading as one! If you enjoy making your own holiday gifts, I guarantee this comely threesome will be well received. It is a gift to be treasured year-round. You may choose to create a single wreath and give it as a tree ornament—or couple it with a small, decorative easel so it can be placed on a bedside table.

MATERIALS LIST

· 9 seashells · 1 white silk hydrangea · 1 green silk hydrangea ·

· 1 spray of artificial forsythia · 6 stems of dried global anthus ·

· 1 bunch of dried pepper berry · 2 sprays of artificial green ivy ·

· 4 red bark dogwood branches · 1 stem of dried horsetail (equisetum)·

· three 6" (xcm) grapevine wreaths · three 13" (33cm) pieces of 1"

(2.5cm) wide double-faced red satin ribbon · 22-gauge wire ·

· floral tape · glue gun ·

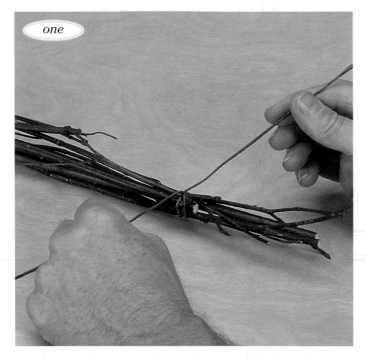

one

two

three

1 Wrap four red bark dogwood branches at each end and at the center with 22-gauge wire wrapped in floral tape. This will be your hanger for the three 6" (15cm) wreaths.

2 Glue a sprig of ivy to the 6" (15cm) wreath. Glue white hydrangea flowers to the ivy.

3 Glue the pepper berries and the green silk hydrangea throughout the wreath. Place the dark hydrangea blossoms on top of the white hydrangea blossoms.

four

4 Cut the forsythia into 2" (5cm) sprigs, and glue them throughout the wreath. Glue the global anthus throughout also.

5 Cut a 13" (33cm) piece of 1"-wide (2.5cm) satin ribbon. Loop it through the wreath and around the four red bark dogwood branches, and glue the overlapped ribbon ends together.

five

NATURAL TWIGS

When working with natural twigs, branches or grape or honeysuckle vines, I recommend spraying them with glossy woodtone spray paint (it's more like a stain). Before spraying slip your hand into a plastic sandwich bag to protect it from the excess paint. Hold the twigs at arm's length and spray them from a distance. The light mist of the spray enriches the veins of the twigs and gives them a new appearance. This process is an excellent way to rejuvenate and recycle old grapevine wreaths.

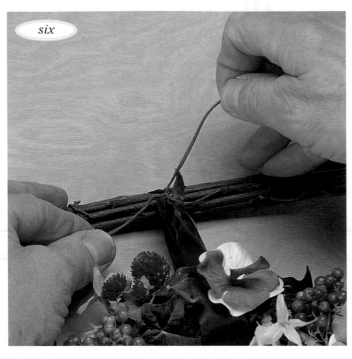

six

6 Wrap a piece of 22-gauge wire with floral tape, then pinch the ribbon together and wrap the wire around the four red bark dogwood branches.

7 Cut a 28" (71cm) piece of ribbon, and tie it in a shoestring bow. Glue on top of the first ribbon.

seven

WORKING WITH DRIED FLOWERS

When drying fresh flowers for a wreath, I rarely allow my flowers to dry to a completely brittle state. The trick I've learned is, they are much easier to arrange and design when they are flaccid rather than brittle. Otherwise the flowers have a tendency to crumble as you use them. Once the project is finished they will complete the drying process in their new situation.

eight

nine

8 Glue three seashells and one green hydrangea blossom to the center of the bow. Repeat steps 2 through 8 for the other two wreaths.

9 Glue the dried horsetail to the red bark dogwood branches.

DESIGNER'S TIP

For the holiday season, you might consider following the age-old tradition of the British Druids. Add sprigs of holly to the existing ivy. In lieu of the forsythia, hydrangea and global anthus, place tiny sprigs of evergreen, additional seashells and accents of miniature ornaments of your choice. Velvet ribbon can replace the satin, and brighter red berries can replace the pepper berries (or the two can be combined). Most important, keep your materials light and airy, allowing the vine wreath to be more than just noticeable.

DOGWOOD LOOKING GLASS

Tabletop treasures rise to a new height of glory when displayed on a mirror plateau. The simplicity of encircled dogwood blossoms enhances a reflection of elegance. Envision this plateau in the center of your dining room table, crowned with a simple three-branch candelabra, the flickering flames reflected in the mirror creating an illusion of a multitude of tiny lights. In a word, "romantic."

MATERIALS LIST

· 2 sprays of silk dogwood blossom branches ·

· 2 sprays of natural birch twigs (about 6 twigs) ·

· sheet moss · 14" (36cm) foam wreath (2" or 5cm deep) ·

· 14" (36cm) mirror · glue gun · floral pins · scissors ·

one

two

three

four

1 Glue the mirror to the foam wreath.

2 Dampen the sheet moss, and attach it along the edge of the wreath with floral pins. Place the pins at a 45° angle.

3 Use scissors to trim the sheet moss along the top and bottom of the wreath.

4 Use floral pins to attach the dogwood branches to the wreath.

five

six

5 Glue a few of the dogwood blossoms to the mirror.

6 Insert six birch branches and secure them with floral pins.

7 Glue one longer branch across one edge of the mirror.

seven

DESIGNER'S TIP

The basic foundation—wreath, frame and mirror—provides inexhaustible decorating possibilities, stretching from a contemporary look to a Victorian flair. Let your imagination run wild! You may create this in a variety of sizes, anywhere from 10" to 24" (24cm to 61cm). Since the mirror is elevated, you can place additional candles on the tabletop as well as the mirror, providing candle glow at more than one level. Consider adding an elegant ribbon in a color that would match your china pattern. Or use a silk flower other than the dogwood to coordinate with your table setting.

ROSE GARLAND

Through myth, folklore and legend, the rose has always appeared as a magical symbol, especially in affairs of the heart. Her colors speak of love, passion, grace and desire, and—when garlanded—roses become a reward of virtue and beauty. For the first and every anniversary following, a garland of roses is sure to keep the magic of romance alive.

MATERIALS LIST

· 12 stems each of silk pink roses, silk white roses and silk red roses ·
12 stems of silk rose buds, 4 in each color · two 43" lengths (109cm) of
1" wide (2.5cm) burgundy double-faced satin ribbon · two 44" lengths
(112cm) of 1½"-wide (4cm) white double-faced satin ribbon ·
· two 41" lengths (104cm) of 1½"-wide (4cm) pink double-faced satin
ribbon · 16" (41cm) foam wreath · 24-gauge paddle wire ·
· floral pins · green spray paint · two 4" (10cm) wire picks ·
· glue gun · chenille stems · floral tape ·

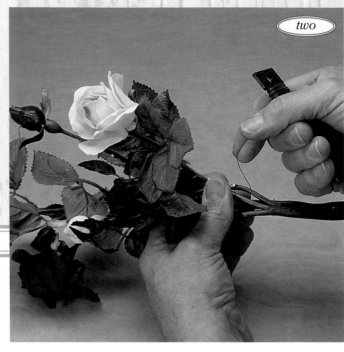

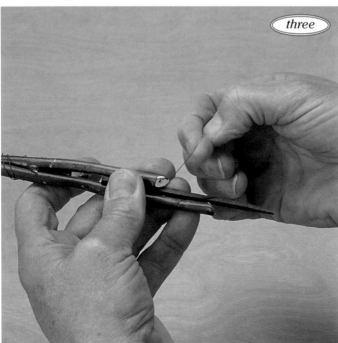

one

two

three

1. Apply green spray paint to the foam wreath. Let dry. Cut the wreath form in half. Set aside one half for another project.

2. Cut the rose sprays into individual sprigs of roses. Use paddle wire to make a 6"-8" long bunch of two pink roses, one red rose, a pink rosebud and a red rosebud. Start wrapping two roses, and keep adding the rest of the roses as you go. Repeat to make a second bunch.

3. Wrap a 4" (10cm) wire pick onto the end of each rose bunch.

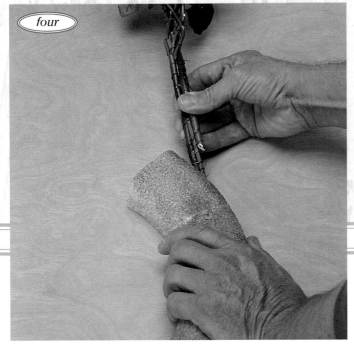

4 Insert the two bunches on either end of the wreath.

5 Insert a rose on either end of the foam wreath to cover the stems of each bunch.

6 Use floral pins to attach 5" to 6" (13cm to 15cm) sprigs of rose leaves along the wreath.

seven

eight

nine

ten

⑦ Cut the remaining roses with about 3" (8cm) stems, and insert them into the wreath, Mix the white, red and pink roses.

⑧ Add rosebuds with about 5" (13cm) stems.

⑨ Cut the pink ribbon to 41" (104cm), the white to 44" (112cm) and the burgundy to 43" (109cm). Fold them so they are staggered, and dovetail the end of each ribbon. Loop the ribbons around the bunch and glue them together. Do not glue the ribbons on top of each other perfectly, but slightly askew. Repeat on the other side of the garland.

⑩ Create a chenille hanger on both ends of the rose garland.

A ROSE BY ANY OTHER NAME…

The rose is the flower of love. Her birth is the most romantic of all myths. It seems Chloris, the Greek goddess of flowers, discovered the body of a lifeless nymph lying in the woods. "I'll transform her into the most beautiful of all flowers," she proclaimed. She called upon Aphrodite, the goddess of love and beauty, to give the nymph beauty; Dionysus, the god of wine, to give nectar for fragrance; and the three graces to notate charm, joy and brilliance. Zephyrus, the west-wind, blew away the clouds, while Apollo, the sun, blessed the new flower with his warmth. The beauty of the new flower was breathtaking and was given the name Rose, the Queen of All Flowers, which she remains to this day!

DESIGNER'S TIP

Display your garland over the guest bed or in the powder room, even among the pots and pans hanging from the pot rack in the kitchen. The laundry room could be wildly enhanced with a colorful garland and probably give a much more exciting reason for going in there. If you have a favorite flower other than the rose, use it to make your garland. Or use a combination of all your favorite flowers … or no flowers at all. Use multiple foliage instead, which will give you the opportunity to dress it up for a variety of occasions. Evergreens, holly and eucalyptus would create a festive garland for the holidays, especially if you trim it with decorative ornaments and/or small wrapped packages. The packages could carry trinkets and fun knickknack gifts for children. Hang it over the fireplace in lieu of the worn-out stockings.

FUNNY VALENTINE

From ancient Greece to the twenty-first century, rose petals have been the symbol of beauty and sweetness of young lovers. Gracefully fashioned into the romantic shape of a heart, rose petals can speak for lovers of all ages: "Be my Valentine." In miniature form, the hearts are perfect for bridal shower gifts or guest favors at the wedding reception.

MATERIALS LIST

· 2 packages of silk rose petals ·

· 5 stems of dried silk rose leaves · 12" (31cm) foam heart frame ·

· 36" (91cm) of 1½"-wide (4cm) double-faced pink satin ribbon ·

· one 3" (8cm) wire pick · 22-gauge floral wire ·

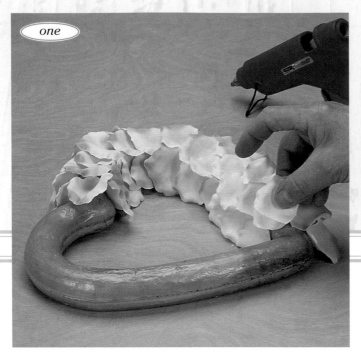

one

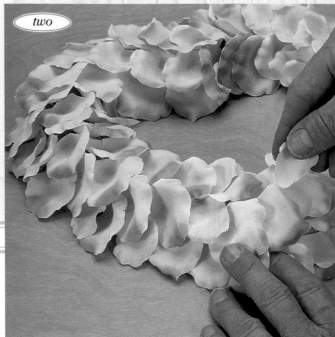

two

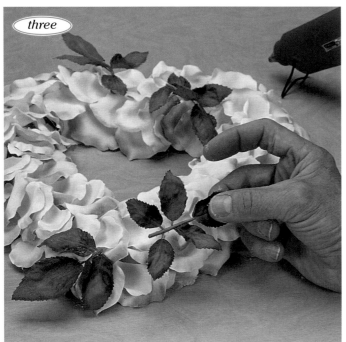

three

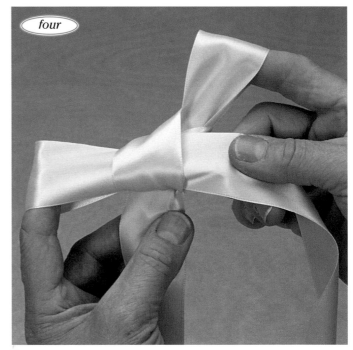

four

① Glue rose petals to the foam heart frame. Cover entirely.

② Glue the smaller rose petals as a filler throughout the wreath.

③ Glue four 5" (13cm) stems of rose leaves to the wreath (two at the bottom and two at the top).

④ Cut 1 yard (91cm) of 1½"-wide (4cm) satin ribbon. Tie a shoe-string bow.

LOVE AND ROSE PETALS

When Cleopatra sailed upstream to rendezvous with Mark Anthony in Cilia, her fabulous barge was covered with rose petals to the depth of two feet. She presented herself on cushions and pillows, which were stuffed with thousands of petals, while the air and all that surrounded her was heavy with perfume. Later, when she beckoned Mark Anthony to her palace, he found the floors carpeted with petals, the banquet tables covered with them, and even the surfaces of the courtyard lakes and pools had changed their color from blue to the ravishing pastels of rose petals. Today, rose petals are scattered at the feet of a bride on her wedding day as a symbol of the beauty and sweetness of young love.

5 Glue the bow to the top of the wreath in between the two leaf stems.

6 Glue on extra rose petals to cover the ends of the rose leaves.

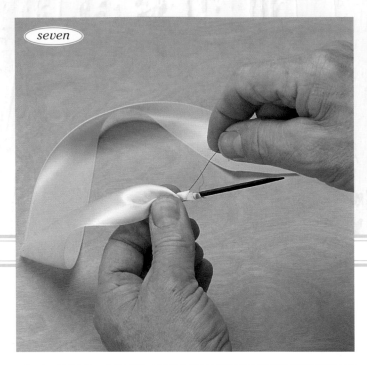

seven

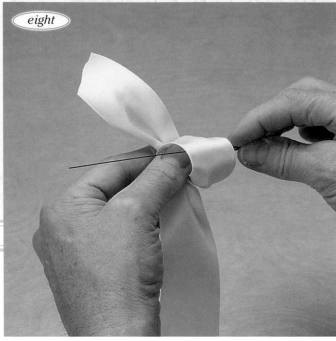

eight

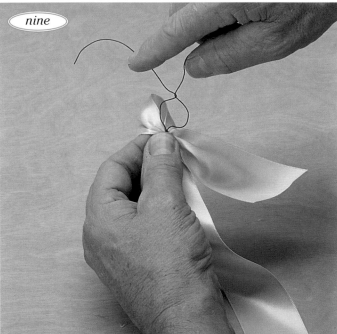

nine

7 To make the hanger, cut an 18" (46cm) strip of ribbon. Wrap a 3" (8cm) wire pick around the ribbon.

8 Make a small loop in the ribbon, and insert a 22-gauge floral wire into the loop.

9 Pull the wire taut, and twist the ends of the wire together. Make a small loop in the wire, and cut off the excess.

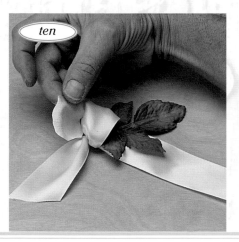

ten

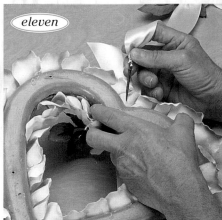

eleven

10 Glue the last leaf stem under the bow loop. Glue one small rose petal to the side of the bow to hide the wire loop hanger.

11 Insert the 18" (46cm) piece of ribbon and wire pick into the back of the wreath at the top of the heart.

DESIGNER'S TIP

A heart of rose petals can quietly welcome a new baby into our world. In the hands of a small child it can precede a bride to the altar, or say, "Ours is a very special relationship," when presented on Mother's Day. An interlocking pair can release an engagement secret and help announce the upcoming wedding.

WEDDING MEMORIES

Long after the words "I do" are softly uttered, treasured moments can linger forever within the hearts of generations to come. What a thoughtful first wedding anniversary gift this makes! Yet this unique and refreshing wall hanger need not be limited to wedding memories. Any picture-perfect moment can be immortalized.

MATERIALS LIST

· 6 dried silk roses · silk baby's breath · 6 pearl sprays · 4 stems of rose leaves · three 6" (15cm) moss-covered, wire-reinforced foam hearts · · 24" (61cm) wood trim, 1¼" (3cm) wide, 18" (46cm) long · 50" (127cm) of 2½"-wide (6cm) velvet ribbon · 30" (76cm) of ⅝"-wide (1cm) grosgrain ribbon · three 30" (76cm) strips of 1½" (4cm) wide double-faced white satin ribbon · 22-gauge wire · straight pins · tacks · · glue gun · hairspray · photos ·

one

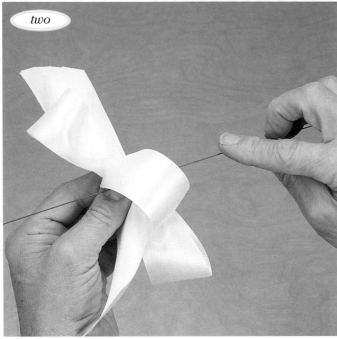

two

1 Cut a 50" (127cm) piece of velvet ribbon, and glue it to the 24" (61cm) wooden trim, allowing a bit of overlap on each end.

2 Cut a 28" (71cm) piece of satin ribbon, and make a bow. Insert a 22-gauge wire into the center of the bow.

3 Cut out a photo, and glue it to one of the heart frames. Glue the bow to the top and center of the heart frame.

three

four

4 Cut four rose leaf sprigs with 4" to 5" (10cm to 13cm) stems. Glue two to either side of the bow on the top, and glue two on the pointed end of the heart. Spray the moss-covered frame with hairspray to prevent shedding.

5 Glue two rosebuds to the heart, one to the top and one to the bottom.

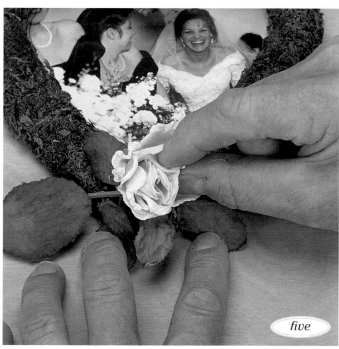

five

THE BEAUTY OF SIMPLICITY

The ancient British considered rosemary a token of happiness. Their young brides carried sprigs in their bridal bouquets to assure them of a faithful husband (a practice that is continued today). However, Anne of Cleves carried an entire bouquet of nothing but rosemary at her wedding to Henry VIII, and we all know what happened to poor Anne. The lesson…never overdo a good thing; less is more, and simplicity is elegance.

six

seven

eight

6 Glue baby's breath to the bottom of the heart. Glue the pearl spray to the top of the heart.

7 Repeat steps 2 through 6 for two more wreaths. Tack the heart wreaths to the wooden frame.

8 To make the hanger, cut a 30" (76cm) piece of grosgrain ribbon, and tie it in a knot at either end. Glue the back of each knot to the top heart.

nine

9 Insert two straight pins into the two knots while the glue is still wet for extra security.

DESIGNER'S TIP

Picture these hearts framing your child's first wide-eyed smile, first efforts at walking, or with a face full of birthday cake! The novelty trim can certainly be replaced— pink for a girl, blue for a boy. Or substitute a fabric tape measure for the ribbon: Pin it on the frame so it can be removed and used to document the baby's growth. Also, nostalgic portraits from the past can create a sentimental grouping that would bring favorite relatives into the twenty-first century. You can have antiquated photos touched up, as well as altered to the necessary size. Take a picture ... give a memory ... they both last longer!

To every thing there is a season, and a time to every purpose under the heaven; a time to be born; and a time to die; a time to plant and a time to pluck up that which is planted.

Ecclesiastes 3:1-2

CELEBRATE
the Seasons

To celebrate the seasons is also to celebrate our purpose and our time that is given. Every season through which we travel in our lifetime is intrinsic unto itself. The birds will sing their songs only one spring, therefore…let us celebrate! The flowers that bloom will fade at summer's end, therefore…let us celebrate! The rich colors of autumn cannot perform an encore, therefore…let us celebrate! The chill of another winter will touch us differently, therefore…let us celebrate! On the pages that follow, I have humbly expressed my praise, glory and honor to the four seasons in a variety of artistic tributes. And with each, I have celebrated my own time in their presence. Follow them step-by-step if you will, the celebrations are ready-made. However, like a spring butterfly you may choose to wing a different flight, allowing your celebrations to be intrinsic unto themselves.

COUNTRY CHORUS

As it takes many blending voices to create the beautiful music of a chorus, so it takes many dried materials blending to create this beautiful wreath. Although every bloom is intrinsic unto itself, dried flowers blended in harmony truly orchestrate a chorus of beauty. Every octave of color, texture, scent and form allows the wreath to reach a glorious crescendo.

MATERIALS LIST

· 6 dried roses · 9 stems of dried yarrow · 4 stems of dried sunflowers ·
· 1 bunch of dried millet · 8 stems of dried dusty miller ·
· 8 pieces (about 6 stems) of dried hydrangea · 10 stems of dried
cockscomb · 1 bunch of prepared eucalyptus · 1 bunch of seeded
eucalyptus · 16" (41cm) foam wreath · green spray paint ·
· glue gun · eight 4" (10cm) wire picks · twenty-eight 3" (8cm)
· wire picks · chenille stem · floral pins · hairspray ·

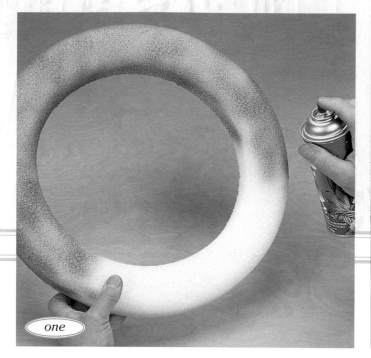

one

two

three

four

1 Spray paint a 16" (40.6cm) foam wreath.

2 Cut 4" to 6" (10cm to 15cm) sprigs of seeded eucalyptus. Insert thirty to thirty-six sprigs sporadically throughout the wreath.

3 Cut thirty to thirty-six sprigs of prepared eucalyptus to 4" to 6" (10cm to 15cm) each. Insert the sprigs sporadically throughout the wreath.

4 Cut ten stems of dried cockscomb in 4" (10cm) sprigs. Insert them into the wreath.

five

six

seven

eight

5 Cut three stems of hydrangea into four smaller pieces with ½" (1cm) stems. Use the floral pins to insert them into the wreath, filling in the holes. The stems can each be glued into the wreath for extra security.

6 Cut three stems of hydrangea into four smaller pieces with 3" (8cm) stems. Attach a 3" (8cm) wire pick to each one. Insert them next to the other hydrangea.

7 Cut eight 4" to 5" (10cm to 13cm) sprigs of dried dusty miller. Attach each sprig to a 3" (8cm) wire pick, and insert them in clusters of two in a V-shape.

8 Cut 15 of the millet stems into 6" (15cm) sprigs. Wrap five clusters, each with three stems of millet, onto a 3" (8cm) wire pick. Insert them in a crisscross fashion.

nine

ten

eleven

twelve

⑨ Cut six stems of yarrow into 3" to 4" (8cm to 10cm) sprigs, and insert them on one side of the wreath.

⑩ Cut the remaining millet stems in half. Create three clusters of five millet stems each, and one cluster of six stems of millet. Wrap each cluster with 4" (10cm) wire picks and floral tape. Repeat using the bottom half of the millet stems to create a total of eight clusters, four with heads and four without heads. Insert the four millet-head clusters to give the illusion of one large cluster.

⑪ Insert the four headless clusters of millet to give the illusion of stems in one long piece.

⑫ Cut four sunflowers right at the head of the flower, and glue them throughout the wreath.

13 Cut six dried roses with 1" (3cm) stems, and glue them into the wreath.

14 Cut three stems of yarrow into 3" (8cm) sprigs, and wrap them together onto a 3" (8cm) wire pick. Insert them into the millet to give the illusion that it is holding the millet in place. Spray the wreath with hairspray to help prevent shedding. Create a hanger with a chenille stem.

DESIGNER'S TIP

If you find it difficult to duplicate this wreath, rest assured that substitutions can be made. Mix and match flowers and foliages, textures and colors, and before you make any final choices, be sure everything will blend together well, and that you are pleased with their harmony. How wonderful it would be to create the Country Chorus with the flowers from your very own garden! I recommend the choices be partially dried before you begin assembly. Simply hang the flowers and foliage upside down in small bunches in a dark, dry area. This is called air-drying. Once they have become soft and pliable, and not completely brittle-dry, you are ready to begin. Follow the steps listed. Keep in mind that color will often alter as the drying process takes place. For example, flowers that are red or purple have a tendency to darken, almost to the point of being black. Experiment in advance with your color choices so you will not be disappointed. You will find selecting the "members" for your "chorus," and testing their unison, is as creative and exciting as the final orchestration.

FOR THE BIRDS

My father used to say, "The songs of birds will always be with you if you keep seed outside your window." So, build it and they will come: a bed-and-breakfast for the birds! With a firm foundation and endless hospitality, a vacancy sign will never appear. Secure it to the trunk of a tree or anchor it to a wooden fence, mailbox or lamppost. It will not only become what I like to call garden art, but every bird in the neighborhood will want to dine at such a fine place.

MATERIALS LIST

· two 6" (15.2cm) birdhouses · 1 spray of silk sunflowers ·

· 1 bunch of pepper berry · 10 red bark dogwood branches ·

· birdseed · sunflower seeds · red spray paint · 2 chenille stems ·

· floral tape · 22-gauge wire · two ⅝" (1cm) screws ·

· Spanish moss · glue gun · cardboard ·

one

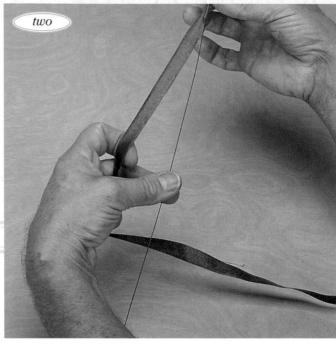

two

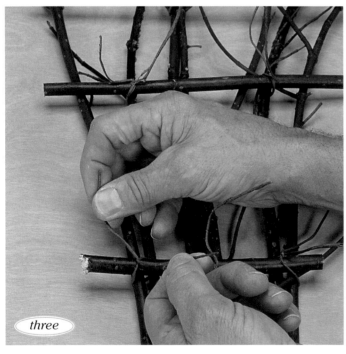

three

1 Spray paint the birdhouses red.

2 Wrap 18" of the 22-gauge wire with floral tape. Repeat for nine pieces of wire.

3 Gather seven red bark dogwood branches 30" to 36" (76cm to 91cm) long each. Fan the branches out. Place an 8" (20cm) branch across the top, a 6" (15cm) branch across the bottom of the fan and a 7" (18cm) branch across the middle. Use the 22-gauge wire wrapped in floral tape to secure all the areas where the branches cross (at least nine spots), creating a trellis of branches.

four

4 Place a ⅝" (1cm) screw into the back and top of each birdhouse.

5 Twist a chenille stem around the screw on each birdhouse, and attach one birdhouse to the 8" (20cm) branch and the other birdhouse to the 7" (18cm) branch. Cut off the ends of the chenille stems.

five

BIRDSEED CAKES

To make a treat the birds in your backyard will really enjoy, try this easy recipe for Birdseed Cakes.

Fats (suet, bacon fat, lard or drippings from roast meat)
Sunflower seeds
Chopped nuts of choice

Combine the fats (all or any combination of them) and mold them into a sizeable ball (like a tennis ball). Roll the ball in the nuts and seeds, creating a thick, heavy covering. Poke a 19-gauge floral wire through the center of the ball. Fashion a hanging hook at the top end of the wire. Attach a twig, horizontally, to the lower end of the wire. Hang in your favorite tree!

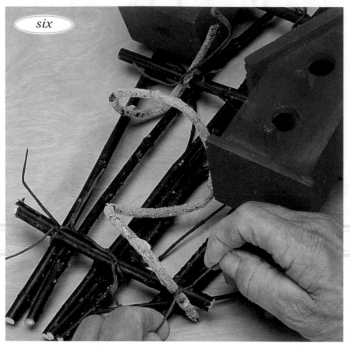

six

seven

eight

nine

6 Cut off the main stem of the sunflower spray, and twist the stem into a corkscrew. Attach it to the 6" (15cm) branch and the 7" (18cm) branch with the 22-gauge wire wrapped in floral tape.

7 Cut five sunflowers from the spray, leaving a stem on each. Use 22-gauge wire wrapped in floral tape to attach the flowers to the frame. Glue the leaves of the sunflowers to the birdhouse.

8 Add three small pieces of red bark dogwood branches. Glue them in front of the birdhouses to add depth.

9 Glue three sprays of pepper berries to the bottom and middle of the branch trellis. Cut off the stems of the pepper berry to 1" (3cm).

[96]

ten

eleven

10 Cut out three cardboard circles to 3" to 4" (8cm to 10cm) in diameter, and glue birdseed and sunflower seeds to it. Glue them to the wreath.

11 Insert Spanish moss into the bird-houses.

DESIGNER'S TIP

Although this trellis could adorn your front or back door, greeting your guests with a touch of whimsy, I suggest you find a more perfect place, like outside your window, as a gift to the birds! You may wish to expand your bed-and-breakfast complex from the very beginning. Create the trellis with larger and stronger branches or wooden strips from the hardware store. The houses are available in different sizes, or you may want to design and build your own. Let the step-by-step instructions guide you, feeling free to render any changes you find necessary, such as using tacks or nails in place of the 22-gauge wire. The seeds in step 10 can be replaced with larger premolded seed balls available at hardware stores and specialty wild bird shops. Use 22-gauge wire to fasten the balls to the trellis. Remember, the more seed, the more song!

GREEN THANKSGIVING GARLAND

A day of thanksgiving can happen anytime. This green Thanksgiving garland was designed purposely, avoiding the traditional theme of bronze and yellow so often thought essential for fall holidays. Green, the neutral color of nature, evokes a sense of quiet and comfort, relaxation and peace. Green garlands, therefore, become inspirational for evoking thanks at any time. And giving thanks should never end.

MATERIALS LIST

· 1 spray of green silk hydrangea · 1 artificial pine willow garland, 54"
(137cm) long · 3 sprays of prepared oak leaf branches ·
· three 14"(36cm) and three 18" (46cm) pheasant feathers ·
· 2 sprays of artificial green viburnum · 2 large pinecones · 1 artificial
wild berry garland, 2-yard (1.8m) long · 3 yards (11m) of 1½"-wide
(3.8cm) double-faced green satin wired ribbon ·
· 22-gauge wire · glue gun ·

TIPS FOR CREATING SILK WREATHS

- Select flowers whose stems can be easily maneuvered and controlled.
- Look for blossoms with individually wired petals. They have the advantage of bending and twisting into a more natural shape.
- For any wreath, even one you prefer to be monochromatic, select flowers in a variety of sizes and shapes, perhaps adding some grasses and/or berries. This gives you the opportunity to have good depth and dimension to your design.
- Remember to keep the blossoms proportioned to the project. Large flowers on a small wreath, for example, will give the wreath a clumsy, heavy appearance. On the other side of the coin, small flowers on a large wreath will become insignificant and lost.
- My best advice is to work strictly with new merchandise. Too many times flowers found at closeout or garage sales are extremely difficult to clean and perk up.

1 Take a 54" (137cm) pine willow garland, and cut it into one yard (91cm). Take a 2-yard (1.8m) piece of wild berry garland, and double it up to make a 1-yard (91cm) section. Wire the wild berry garland to the pine willow garland.

2 Thin out the three sprigs of oak leaves for a natural look. Use 22-gauge wire to attach it to the garland.

3 Attach two sprays of viburnum to the garland with 22-gauge wire.

four

five

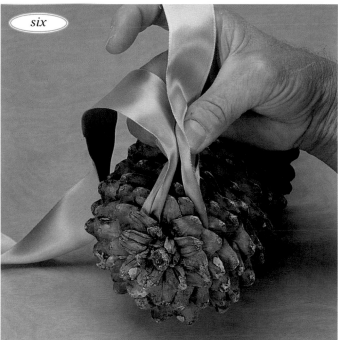

six

4 Attach three sprigs of hydrangea with 22-gauge wire to the garland. This is the focal point. Cut off the excess and glue on a few of the green prepared oak leaves.

5 Glue three 14" (35cm) and three 18" (46cm) pheasant feathers to the garland.

6 Cut two 1-yard (91cm) pieces of green ribbon. Fold the ribbon lengthwise, place around the bottom of the pinecone and glue the ribbon together. Repeat on the other pinecone.

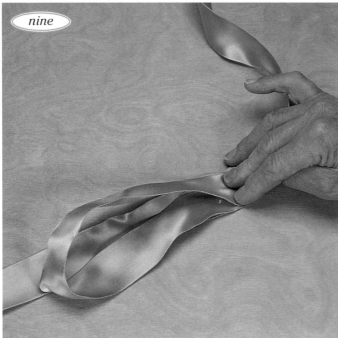

7. Cut four oak leaves off the stem, and glue two on the bottom of each pinecone. Cut two small sprigs of wild berries, and glue each on the center of the oak leaves.

8. Tie the pinecones to the garland with the green ribbon.

9. Cut 1 yard (91cm) of ribbon, fold it to make a loop and glue it.

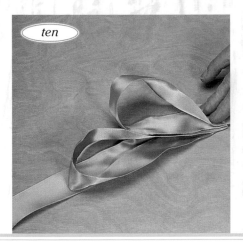

ten

eleven

10 Fold the ribbon into another loop and glue it again.

11 Glue the top of the bow to the garland. Add a 22-gauge wire hanger and place it in the center, where the weight of the wreath is. Create two hangers to help distribute the weight.

DESIGNER'S TIP

Jump-start the holiday and display your garland early. Once the turkey feast is over and the platter is stored away, the garland can remain, announcing the arrival of the next holiday season. If you're not partial to a green garland, you can opt to revert back to the old-fashioned colors, but give yourself a chance to enjoy the risk of being different. After all, that's what creativity is all about.

ORANGE DELIGHT

Exuberance, joviality, vigor and boldness ring loud and clear with the color orange; orange will add intensity to any décor. Setting such a mood can be easily achieved, even with the frailty of Japanese lanterns. For the Christmas holidays, pinecones, small and equal in size, combined with rose hips (or bright red artificial berries) and accented with a green or red plaid ribbon, would make delightful gifts!

MATERIALS LIST

· 6 bunches of dried Japanese lantern pods ·

· 1 bag of dried rose hips · 12" (31cm) wire-reinforced wreath ·

· 1 yard (91cm) of 2½"-wide (6cm) double-faced red satin

ribbon · chenille stem · glue gun · 22-gauge wire ·

1. Glue Japanese lantern pods around the 12" (31cm) wire reinforced wreath. Put hot glue on the wreath rather than the pods, and allow the glue to dry somewhat before carefully placing the pods, so they won't break.

2. Put a little hot glue in between the pods, and sprinkle rose hips into the wreath.

3. Cut 1 yard (91cm) of 2½"-wide (6cm) ribbon, and create a small loop for the center of the bow and two larger loops to form the bow.

four

five

4. Insert 22-gauge wire into the small center loop and twist to secure. Cut off the excess wire.

5. Insert the bow just to the left of center, and create a chenille stem loop to hang the wreath.

DESIGNER'S TIP

The Japanese lanterns can be replaced with another material should their color or frailty cause concern. Try miniature artificial fruit. You can achieve the same tight and tufted effect of the lanterns with limes, for example. Their shapes are almost identical. Instead of the rose hips, if you prefer, use tiny white silk blossoms (baby's breath perhaps), and accent the wreath with a bright lemon-yellow ribbon. Your finished wreath will manifest a summertime flare! Whatever you choose to replace the lanterns with, they need to be small and about the same size. Should you desire to use larger fruit, be sure to start with a larger wreath frame.

WINTER BLUE

The color blue can actually help warm up the celebration of the winter season. Nonthreatening, blue is known as the color of trust, and therefore gives a solemn promise that spring will soon return. If yew trees don't live in your area, substitute a collection of evergreens. For the best winter look, select the darkest green possible.

MATERIALS LIST

· 16" (40cm) wire-reinforced foam wreath · 5 artificial red berry sprays ·
· 3 artificial blueberry sprays · 6 pinecones · yew · 2 bunches of dried
blue eucalyptus pods · ¼-yard (23cm) of 45"-wide (114cm)
cotton fabric · floral pins · wood tone spray paint · green spray paint ·
· 24-gauge paddle wire · eleven 4" (10.2cm) wire picks ·
· 22-gauge wire · wire clothes hanger ·

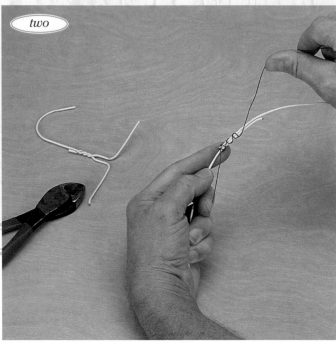

1 Spray the 16" (40.6cm) wreath with green spray paint. Insert 3" to 5" (8cm to 13cm) sprigs of yew into the wreath. Cover it entirely.

2 Cut the hanger apart, and use the paddle wire to create a circle that fits inside the wreath.

3 Cut 3" to 4" (8cm to 13cm) sprigs of blue eucalyptus pods, and use the paddle wire to attach them to the hanger. Cover it entirely.

four

five

six

4) Cut 3" (8cm) off the blueberry spray stems. Insert three sprays into the foam, and use the floral pins to secure them along the wreath.

5) Use 22-gauge wire from underneath the wreath, and twist it around the wreath and blue eucalyptus pod ring. Repeat three times to secure.

6) Use wood tone spray paint to tone down the bright red berries. Allow to dry.

7 Wrap each red berry spray onto a 4" (10cm) wire pick. Insert five berry sprays into the wreath, evenly spaced.

8 Wrap a 22-gauge wire around the base of a pinecone and twist to create a stem. Repeat on five more pinecones.

9 Wrap 4" (10cm) wire picks around the pinecone stems created in step 8. Insert the pinecones into the wreath.

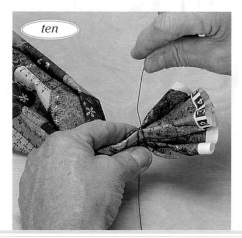

ten

eleven

10 Fold the cotton fabric into thirds. Fold the raw edge in. Gather each end of the fabric, and wrap a 22-gauge wire around each end.

11 To create the hanger, place the fabric through the wreath, loop it together, and fold the ends in to create a puff. Twist a 22-gauge wire around it to secure.

DESIGNER'S TIP

During cold temperatures, the evergreens will remain fresh as the wreath hangs on your front or back door. Think about making a matching wreath to place on the mailbox, and even a third wreath to adorn the lamppost. Display them after Thanksgiving and adorn with a few sprigs of holly, and your outdoor Christmas decorating job is complete. Come January, remove the faded holly. Tuck a bird's nest among the boughs, encouraging an early spring arrival. If the color blue presents a problem, the eucalyptus pods can be replaced with white tallow berries, or the burnt orange of rose hips. The yellow-gold of dried yarrow or the red-violet of heather give you two additional options. Of course, whatever color choice you make, be sure to coordinate your fabric hanger. But no one's saying you can't hang all your wreaths with discarded yet colorful neckties.

GLAD PLAID CHRISTMAS

The first ribbons were believed to have been made in France as early as the IIth century, woven on handlooms one at a time. Today they are considered the perfect finishing touch to almost every holiday decoration, especially the Christmas wreath. Graceful loops among the boughs create a never-ending circle of gladness.

MATERIALS LIST

· 16" (41cm) foam wreath · 25 yards (22.9m) of 1¼"-wide (3cm) plaid ribbon · 15 yards (13.7m) of 1¼"-wide (3cm) red ribbon · 40" (102cm) of 2½"-wide (6cm) plaid ribbon · 10 yards (9.2m) of ¼"-wide (1cm) green ribbon · 3 bunches of red berries · 14½" (37cm) artificial pine garland · 14½" (37cm) artificial ivy garland · green spray paint · · forty-eight 3" (8cm) wire picks · three 4" (10cm) wire picks · floral pins · straight pins · green chenille stems · 22-gauge wire · glue gun ·

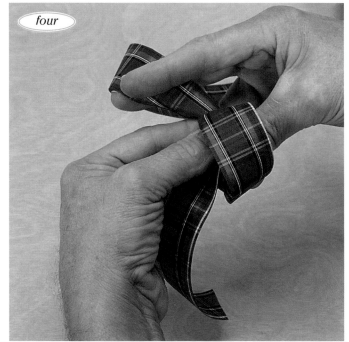

1 Spray the 16" (40.6cm) foam wreath with green spray paint.

2 Use the floral pins to attach the artificial pine garland around the foam wreath. Place the pins at a 45° angle to secure.

3 Cut an 18" (46cm) piece of floral wire into three 6" (15cm) pieces. Cut a 44" (112cm) piece of 1¼"-wide (3cm) plaid ribbon, roll it over and pinch it together.

4 Loop the ribbon while pinching it between your thumb and forefinger. Make a loop above the center.

five

DRYING LEAVES

If you'd like to dry your own wreath, I know an easy way to handle the inevitable curling leaves you have when drying flowers. I place the individual leaves flat on a piece of cardboard and sandwich them with a cardboard topper. Add books to provide weight assuring me the leaves will not be able to move. The pressing time takes about two weeks. Galax leaves work well with this method of drying. I use Galax leaves quite often in my design work. Sometimes I prefer air drying them after I have soaked them in a solution of two parts water and one part liquid floor polish. As the leaves dry, the wax not only adds shine, but also allows them to remain soft and pliable.

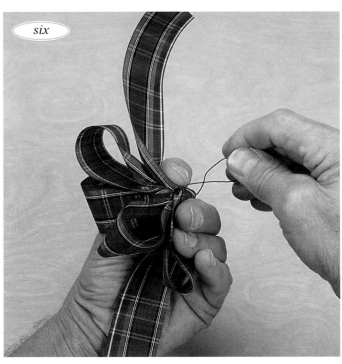

six

5 Make two more loops above the center and two loops under the center. Insert a 6" (15cm) piece of floral wire into the center.

6 Twist the ends of the wire together to secure the bow. Pull the wire taut and twist.

7 Take a 3" (7cm) wire pick and twist it around the bow.

8 Repeat steps 4 through 7 to make twelve bows using the 1¼"-wide (3cm) plaid ribbon and twelve bows with the 1¼"-wide (3cm) red ribbon. Using 28" (71cm) pieces of ribbons, follow the same process to make bows with two loops rather than four. Make twelve two-loop bows each with the ¼"-wide (1cm) green ribbon and the 2½"-wide (6cm) plaid ribbon. Insert the bows into the foam wreath.

9 Twist the 4" (10cm) wire picks around the berry bunches. Wrap the wire of the pick around the base of the berries and the stick to secure. Insert three bunches at a 45° angle into the floral foam wreath.

ten

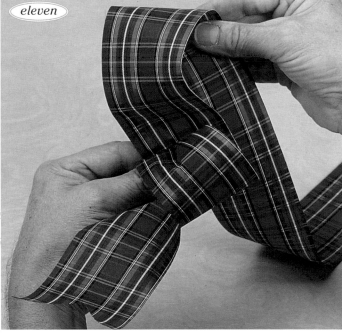

eleven

twelve

10 Cut ivy leaves from an ivy garland. Glue the leaves randomly throughout the wreath.

11 To make the hanger, use the 2½"-wide (6cm) plaid ribbon to make a two-loop bow. Leave a streamer that is dove-tailed.

12 Insert a chenille stem through the center of the bow.

13 Twist the ends of the chenille stems together.

14 Cut off the excess chenille stems. Glue two ivy leaves to the bow, one leaf on each loop of the bow.

15 Cut off the stems of two berries, and glue the berries to each ivy leaf on the bow loops.

16 Fold the end of the ribbon on the bow, making a double fold.

17 With four straight pins, pin the folded section of the bow (your hanger) to the back of the wreath. Place the pins at each of the four corners of the folded ribbon at 45° angles so that all of the pins point toward the center.

DESIGNER'S TIP

Gladness certainly is not limited to just one season. A simple change of ribbon and color combinations, and your wreath can be used to celebrate any time of joy and merriment. Decorate for spring or the Easter holiday by simply replacing the red and green ribbons with pastel colors (perhaps polka dots or even stripes). The ivy is a perfect all-season foundation, but substitute the berries with ornamental eggs, and/or artificial cherry blossoms. Ribbon loops of bright primary colors are wonderful for summertime gladness, especially when paired with miniature birds and birdhouses, butterflies and artificial field daisies. For the fall and Thanksgiving season, use rich colors of the earth—gold, bronze, burnt red. Nestle oak leaves of orange and yellow among the ivy leaves along with accents of natural or artificial bittersweet and acorns. With so many creative combinations, this wreath could easily be retitled, "A Glad Plaid Any Time." Go for it!

JEWELED RAIN

The illusion of spun gold catches and then releases a downpour of jewel-colored ribbon streamers. The crownlike design of regal simplicity and grace is the perfect touch for any royal celebration.

MATERIALS LIST

· 1½ bunches of fresh corkscrew willow branches (sometimes referred to as curly willow) · 6 to 8 gold pinecones · gold spray paint ·
· 4 yards (3.7m) each of ⅜"-wide (1cm) picot-edged purple ribbon, pink ribbon, blue ribbon, green ribbon and hot pink ribbon ·
· 4 yards (3.7m) each of ³⁄₁₆"-wide (.47cm) picot-edged red and turquoise ribbon · 9 holiday ornaments · 22-gauge wire ·

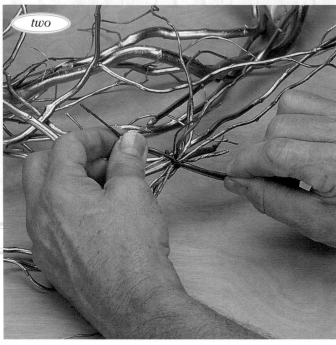

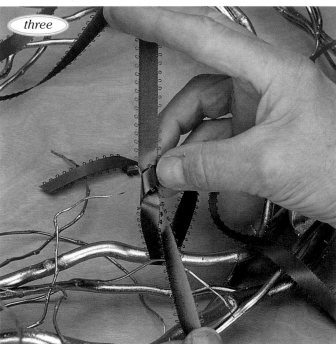

1 Spray gold paint on the corkscrew willow branches. Allow to dry.

2 Twist the corkscrew willow into a wreath and twist a 22-gauge wire around the branches to secure. Weave the branches. Do not cut the wire ends until finished so it can be used multiple times.

3 Cut twenty-one 42" (107cm) strips of picot ribbon: three of each of the seven colors. Knot the ends of each of the ⅜" strips, and tie them in double knots on the corkscrew willow branches. Tie each of the ⅜" ribbon to two different branches on the willow with one streamer longer than the others and a swag in the middle.

4 Knot the ends of the red and turquoise ribbon strips, and tie them in shoestring bows to the corkscrew willow wreath.

five

six

5 Glue the gold pinecones throughout the wreath.

6 Tie four ornaments to the ends of the picot ribbon. Cut five 18" (46cm) strips of ribbon (any color), and tie five more ornaments to the wreath.

DESIGNER'S TIP

The benefit of this wreath is your control of its size and shape. If you have concerns about twisting the willow branches, you can replace them with a purchased grapevine or twig wreath. Try to select one that is not so tightly woven. Spray paint it gold. Keep in mind that if you use something other than the willow branches, your finished project will be somewhat different in appearance because of the firmness of the purchased wreath. Another benefit of this wreath is your option to nestle fresh sprigs of evergreens and holly among the willow branches and around the cones. If they dry before the end of the holiday, simply remove them and replace with fresh. That wonderful holiday fragrance is a big plus!

RESOURCES

The materials used in this book should be available in your local craft and hobby stores. If you have trouble finding them, contact your local florist. Many florists have supplies available for sale or can direct you to a local source for materials. Another great source for supplies is the Internet. Many of the large national craft stores offer online shopping.

"The Perfect Toolkit" available on my Web site includes several of the tools you'll need to create arrangements in your own home. These high-quality tools are American-made. The four-piece kit includes a high leverage floral/craft shear, wire cutter, ribbon shear, and knife. For more information, or to order a kit, visit www.americasflowerman.com.

INDEX

CREATE GORGEOUS WREATHS & FLORALS WITH NORTH LIGHT BOOKS!

These books and other fine North Light craft titles are available from your local art & craft retailer, bookstore, online supplier or by calling 1-800-448-0915.

Make your holidays brighter and more special by creating your very own floral decor! Cele Kahle shows you how to create a variety of gorgeous arrangements, swags, topiaries, wreaths and even bows. There are 19 creative projects in all, using silk foliage, berries, fruit and ribbon. Each one comes with materials lists, step-by-step guidelines and beautiful full-color photos.

ISBN 1-58180-259-5, paperback, 128 pages, #32124-K

Here are 20 beautiful wreath projects, perfect for brightening up a doorway or celebrating a special time of year. You'll find a range of sizes and styles utilizing a variety of creative materials, including dried herbs, sea shells, cinnamon sticks, silk flowers, Autumn leaves, Christmas candy and more. Clear, step-by-step instructions ensure beautiful, long lasting results every time!

ISBN 1-58180-239-0, paperback, 144 pages, #32015-K

Capture the essence of the seasons with these simple, stunning floral arrangements. With a few basic techniques, a handful of materials and a little creativity, you can make eye-pleasing accents for every room in your home. You'll find all the flower arranging advice you need inside, along with 15 projects using silk flowers, greenery, leaves, pinecones, gourds and more.

ISBN 1-58180-108-4, paperback, 96 pages, #31810-K

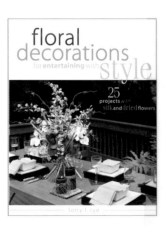

Whether you're planning a grand Thanksgiving dinner, a tropical theme party, or a romantic dinner for two, you'll find a wealth of creative silk and dried floral projects inside-each one designed to make your special occasions stand out. Terry Rye makes creating centerpieces easy, affordable and fun. The results are simply magnificent!

ISBN 1-55870-598-8, paperback, 128 pages, #70537-K